Fruit Infused Water

80 Vitamin Water Recipes for Weight Loss, Health and Detox Cleanse

By

Patrick Smith

ISBN-10: 1500416371
ISBN-13: 978-1500416379

Contents

Fruit Infused Water

When you wake up in the morning, your body is dehydrated and craves water more than anything else. However, sodas and juices don't provide what you need, even if juice has a lot of health benefits.

Avoiding sodas and other sugary drinks is an important step to a healthy lifestyle, but few people want to give up on flavored beverages altogether. The best way to accomplish get taste, vitamins and water in one package is infuse water with fruits in a particular way.

This so-called fruit infused water is the perfect replacement for other beverages, allowing for many varieties that can bring a new taste every day.

How to Make Fruit Infused Water

One of the best things about making fruit infused water is that it is easy to make. As you can see from the photo, all you really need to do is fill a jar, pitcher or bottle with water and add sliced foods, herbs and ice.

It only takes few minutes, so you can make two or three different jars at a time and give yourself several options to choose from. Most waters last up to 3-5 days, if they are kept in the refrigerator.

If you do not want to have fruit and herb pieces in your drink, place a wire strainer at the mouth of your glass, then pour the water.

Fruits

As the name suggests, fruits are the main ingredients in making fruit infused water. Choose good quality fruits as much as possible. Ripe fruits make a sweet drink, so there is no need to ad artificial sweetener. Fortunately, many groceries offer small precut fruits.

Take advantage of fruits that are in season in order to get them fresh. Remember that fruits that are not in season can taste sour or flavorless. In this case, you can go for dried or frozen fruits as well.

Always wash your fruits thoroughly. Pay special attention in cleaning citrus and berries. Organic, unprocessed foods are always the healthiest, so try to get organic fruits as much as possible to minimize the amount of contaminants and pesticides in them.

Herbs

Herbs can change the flavor of your water. Add only a small amount of herbs at the beginning and gradually add them as necessary. This gives you more control over the flavor.

Herbs are optional in most fruit infused water recipes but they often complement the fruits very well. Use whatever herbs are available to you and experiment with them. Mint is the most popular choice for fruit infused water, but you can also try basil, rosemary, thyme and lavender.

Glass pitcher

Be sure to have different pitcher sizes. Jars with 1 and 2 quarts are essential to make sure that you can create different batches. Having large containers also allows you to prepare more water, so you don't have to make more all the time.

Fruit infusion water bottle

There are portable bottles specifically made to hold fruit infused water. Purchasing this product is optional but can be very practical if you travel a lot.

Water

You can use tap water if you are sure it is clean. However, you should always go for high quality water, as it is the healthiest.

Benefits of Fruit Infused Water

Water is considered the best elixir for health and beauty. By infusing it with fruits, you add vitamins, minerals and antioxidants to your drink. Here are some of the health benefits in drinking think kind of water.

Maintains the balance of body fluids

The human body is composed of 60% water. Water helps in digestion, circulation, and the transportation of nutrients in your body.

Whenever your body is low in fluids, it triggers the sensation commonly known as thirst. Unknown to most people, thirst is experienced about 45 minutes after the fluid level gets too low and your concentration has been suffering ever since.

This is why kids should be allowed to drink water in class, because if they get thirsty, they have not been able to concentrate all that well for 45 minutes.

You should always listen to this cue of your body and drink fluids immediately.

Controls calorie intake

Believe it or not, thirst often gets mistaken for hunger. This is why many dieters swear by drinking water as part of their weight loss routine. If you feel hungry, but haven't had a drink in a while, better have a drink before deciding to eat something.

Substituting fruit infused water for sodas and energy drinks also reduce your calorie intake and lead to automatic weight loss. Water is also healthier and more filling than other sugary beverages.

Water energizes the muscle

Cells that do not have enough liquid tend to degenerate, which leads to muscle fatigue. Muscle cells need liquid to perform properly.

When you are exercising, you should give your water consumption special attention. It is a good idea to drink 1 pint (1/2 liter) of fruit infused water before exercising.

Fruit infused water is also great to drink in between workout in order to replace lost fluid.

Keeps skin looking good

Dehydration can affect your skin health and makes the skin look wrinkled and dry. The skin acts as a barrier and protection against external elements. It also prevents excessive fluid loss.

Drinking water infused with tropical fruits and citrus fruits is particularly healthy for your skin. It can prevent wrinkles by locking the moisture in.

Helps the kidneys

Fluids transport waste products away from the cells, while the kidney is primarily responsible for cleaning the body of toxins. One of the signs that you are getting enough liquid is if your urine flows freely and light in color. Once the body is not getting enough water, your urine becomes dark and odorous.

Drinking water helps the kidney to function properly more than any other drink. It can also prevent kidney stones.

Maintains normal bowel movement

You can prevent constipation by drinking enough water. If the body does not get enough liquid, it has to compensate by pulling water from the stool, making it difficult to perform normal bowel function. By infusing your water with fruits that are rich in fiber, you can help the body clean your colon.

Increase your strength

Many detox diets strongly recommend drinking fruit infused water, since it reduces your sugar intake from coffee, soda and juice.

By replacing processed foods and drinks and substituting them with natural fruits and vegetables, you get an energy boost.

Removes excess waste

One of the primary benefits of drinking fruit infused water is to remove excess waste from your body. Cleansing the colon is an important factor in any detox process, because it eliminates harmful chemicals and toxins in your body.

Drinking fruit infused water complements detox programs and makes it easier for your body to adjust to the process.

Strengthens the immune system

Drinking citrus infused water can increase the body's ability to absorb nutrients. Many of the herbs included in fruit infused water recipes also play a big role in keeping your lymphatic system healthy.

The best fruits for strengthening the immune system are those rich in Vitamin C.

Better breath

Coffee and alcohol have very strong odor and cause bad breath. This can be prevented by drinking fruit infused water.

Believe it or not, a dirty colon is often the cause for bad breath. Since drinking fruit infused water can help clean the colon, it also has a positive effect on your breath.

Lighter feeling

People often feel lighter after switching to fruit infused water. This is mainly because water and the fruits used in most recipes contain little to no calories.

It is also free from artificial flavor and processed chemicals that can could upset the stomach.

Improved sense of well being

Most people feel good about making a healthy change in their lifestyle. Drinking healthier beverages improves your wellbeing and can also make you feel better about yourself. This boost in motivation might just get you to make more changes and become even healthier.

Prevents injuries

Making sure that you are getting enough water can prevent cramps and sprain injuries. Liquid ensures that the joints and muscles are well lubricated and that they are elastic enough to prevent muscle pain and fatigue.

Drinking fruit infused water with mint can help to relieve migraine and headache, which is commonly linked to dehydration.

Save money

Water is generally cheaper than soda and coffee. You will also need few fruits and herbs. The cost of making your own flavored water is cheaper than any other beverage.

Great for entertaining

Fruit flavored water is very popular among my guests and some even prefer it over regular soda and juice.

Make a variety of flavored waters for your next party and offer it to your family and friends. These drinks are healthy, inexpensive and refreshing.

Improves cognitive function

Remember that the brain needs a lot of oxygen to function properly. Studies show that drinking at least 10 cups of water a day improves your mental performance by as much as 30%.

Drinking water also supports the nerve function of the brain. The electrolytes remain high and allow the nerves to communicate effectively with each other.

Reduces boredom

It is natural to crave drinks that have flavor. Adding fruits and herbs infuses a hint of flavor into your drink without adding artificial flavoring. This allows you to enjoy a wide variety of flavored waters and prevents you from getting bored with it. This keeps you from returning to unhealthier beverages.

Reduces the risk of cancer

Several cancers are related to your digestive health. Studies show that drinking enough water can reduce the risk of bladder and colon cancer. Water dilutes the cancer causing agents in the body and flushes them out.

Increases metabolism

Drinking plain water can already increase your metabolism. This effect can be intensified by adding citrus fruits into your drink.

Reduces risk of heart attack

Studies show that people who drink enough water are less likely to have a heart attack. Most other beverages are processed, they have sugars and trans fats that are known to clog arteries and increase the risk for heart disease.

Section 1: Metabolism Boosting

Fruits that are high in Vitamin C are a great drink to increase your metabolism. Try these fruit infused water recipes for weight loss.

1. Strawberry and Tangerine Water

This strawberry and tangerine water is easy to make. It is particularly great as quick refreshment while exercising.

½ cup dried or fresh strawberries (sliced)
1 quart (1 liter) water
¼ tsp Rind of tangerine

This drink can be served hot or cold. There are three ways to make it.

For a hot drink, place the strawberries and tangerine in a teapot and cover it with 1 quart of water. Bring to a boil. Cover the nose of the teapot with a mesh then pour the tea into a cup.

For a cold drink, boil 3 cups of water, add the tangerine rind and 1 tsp strawberry. Set aside for three minutes then remove the strawberry. Add cold water and ice.

2. Blueberry Pineapple Water

Pineapple blueberry infused water is good to drink in the morning. The blueberry infuses color and flavor while the pineapple adds the right amount of sweetness. Pineapple also contains a high amount of Vitamin C.

½ cup ice
1/3 cup frozen blueberries
½ cup pineapple chunks
1 quart (1 liter) water

Place the fruits in a pitcher. Add the ice. This is an important step whether you want to serve the water cold or at room temperature, since ice holds the fruit better to infuse the flavor.
Place in the refrigerator or set aside at room temperature an hour before serving. Pour half a cup into your glass then fill with additional water.

3. Apple Cinnamon Tea

This fruit infused tea tastes delicious and will also warm you up.

2 cinnamon sticks
1 sweet apple
2 quarts (2 liters) water

Place sliced apple and 1 cinnamon stick in a tea pot and cover with water. Bring to a boil, then serve in a tea cup or travel cup with 1 extra cinnamon stick.
Note: Do not use cinnamon power as a substitute for sticks, as they will not dissolve.

4. Cranberry Clementine Water

This fruit infused water reminds me of autumn beauty. It has a taste of pepper corns and the sweetness of clementine and pears.

1 thinly sliced pear
1 tbs dried cranberries
1 cut clementine
1 tsp all spice berries
1.5 quarts (1.5 liters) water

Slice the fruits as thinly as possible to release their flavors. You can add another apple, if you want it sweeter. Place the fruits in a pitcher then cover with water and ice. Set aside for at least 3 hours before serving.

5. Grapefruit Sage Water

Grapefruit is known to reduce the insulin levels in the body which can also trigger weight loss. Grapefruit can interact with several medications so you have to consult your doctor before adding it in your diet. Sage also promotes weight loss and even improves your hair condition.

1 cup grapefruit
2 tsp sage
1 quart (1 liter) Water

Wash and drain the grapefruit. Add in a pitcher then mash to breakdown the fruit. Grind the sage then add to the grapefruit. Add sparkling water and set aside for an hour before serving.

6. Blueberry Pomegranate Water

This fruit infused water is rich in antioxidants from the pomegranate and blueberries. It tends to taste better when made with sparkling water.

1 pint fresh blueberries
2 quarts (2 liters) filtered spring water
1 pomegranate

Remove the seeds from the pomegranate. Do this by slicing it into four pieces, then submerging into a bowl of cold water.
The seeds will fall in the bottom. Strain, then add the blueberries to the pomegranate seeds. Place in a pitcher, add cold water and ice. Set aside and wait for 3 hours before serving.

7. Pomegranate Mint Water

The pomegranate and mint add a lot of color and taste to the water.

½ cup mint leaves
1 quart (1 liter) water
¼ cup pomegranate seeds

Combine the ingredients in a pitcher, then place inside the refrigerator for 4 hours to let the flavors infuse. Serve with crushed ice if desired.

8. Blueberry Raspberry Water

Raspberry is one of the fruits that increases metabolism. It enables the body to burn more fat as fuel. Blueberries also act as a powerful antioxidant.

½ cup raspberries
½ cup blueberries
1 pint (½ liter) filtered water

Wash the berries and place them at the bottom of a bottle or pincher. Add the water then mash the berries to release the flavor. You can also refrigerate them for 1 hour. Shake to mix the flavor and serve.

9. Blueberry Coconut water

Coconut is one of the healthiest foods available, having over a hundred health benefits and uses.

½ cup blueberries
1 pint coconut water

Add the berries at the bottom of a pitcher then mash using a spatula. Add the coconut water then stir to infuse the flavor. Place in the refrigerator for 2 hours before serving.

10. Lemon Mint Water

Lemon is one of the most popular citrus fruits that can increase a person's metabolism.

1 gallon (3.75 liters) water
10 sprigs mint
6 lemons, zested and seeded

Combine the water, lemon, and zest in a pincher. Add the cold water and allow it to steep for 6 hours. Remove the lemon and mint. Strain using a mesh.
Pour the water into a glass then garnish with lemon slice. Serve cold.

11. Apple Pomegranate Lemon Water

This fruit infused water is rich in content and flavor. It can be served hot or cold.

3 sliced apples
½ cup chopped rosemary
2 juiced lemons
1 gallon (3.75 liters) water
3 muddled pomegranates
20 pomegranate seeds

Combine the sliced apples and pomegranate seeds with the water and rosemary. Set aside for 6 hours. You can also place it in the refrigerator.
Strain using a fine mesh and fill into a pitcher. Add lemon juice and garnish with pomegranate seeds, rosemary and apple slices.

12. Pear Ginger Water

Pears can promote weight loss and reduce cholesterol levels in the body. Also, they are quite versatile. You can cook, poach and bake them. Naturally, they make a great ingredient for fruit infused water.

10 sliced pears
1 gallon (3.75 liters) water
½ cup peeled and sliced ginger

Combine the ingredients in a container then steep for 6 hours. Strain to have clear water. Pour in a container. Garnish with pear slice and ginger. Serve.

13. Fennel Tangerine Water

Tangerine introduces a great citrus flavor into the water. It also contains a high amount of Vitamin C.

1 gallon (3.75 liters) water
2 shaved fennel bulbs
8 thyme sprigs
12 tangerines, zested and pith removed

Combine all of the ingredients in a pitcher then place in the refrigerator for 6 hours. Strain using a fine mesh. Serve.

14. Cherry Water

Cherries can help your body to use sugar in the blood. Cherries are also rich in anthocyanin, which helps to oxidize body fat.

1.5 pints (710 ml) water
1 lemon slice
3 mint leaves
5 pitted cherries

Mix all of the ingredients and place them in a pitcher. Smash the contents using a spoon or fork. Set aside for 15 minutes or place in the refrigerator to have a cold drink. Serve.

15. Honeydew Mint Water

The natural sweetness of a honeydew melon is perfect if you are craving candy or other sugary indulgences.

½ honeydew melon, cubed
1 lb (450 g) seedless watermelon, cubed
1 cantaloupe, cubed
½ cup fresh mint leaves
1 quart (1 liter) water

Scoop the honeydew melon, watermelon and cantaloupe in a large pitcher. Add the water and stir. Refrigerate for 1 hour. Serve with ice. You can also garnish it with sliced fruits of your choice.

16. Vanilla Orange Water

Oranges and vanilla are perfect to create a delicious and refreshing drink.

2 quarts (2 liters) water
½ tsp vanilla extract
1 sliced orange

Combine the orange slices, water and vanilla in a pitcher. Mix the contents well and let it steep for 1 hour to release the flavors. Serve.

17. Lavender Kiwi Water

Kiwi has a very refreshing flavor that can add a taste of sweetness without being too overpowering. The lavender balances the flavor wonderfully.

4 ripe kiwis
2 tbs crushed lavender leaves
2 quarts (2 liters) water

Wash the kiwis, then cut into thick slices. Place at the bottom of a pitcher then pour the water. Add the lavender then refrigerate for 3 hours. Strain the liquid using a fine clean mesh before serving. Add ice if desired.

18. Raspberry Orange Water

Raspberry and citrus fruits can blend their flavors wonderfully to create a delicious and refreshing drink. Choose an orange that is naturally sweet in order for the water to be sweet as well. Avoid using artificial sweeteners.

1 orange
2 quarts (2 liters) water
2 cups raspberries

Wash the raspberries and smash lightly using a fork. Thinly slice the orange. Place the fruits at the bottom of a pitcher, then add the water. Refrigerate overnight for best results. Serve with garnish and ice if desired.

19. Lime Mint Water

Lime infused water is a good metabolism booster, because it contains a lot of Vitamin C. This recipe also incorporates mint to add a refreshing flavor.

2 limes
2 quarts (2 liters) sparkling water
½ cup mint

Slice the lime into thick pieces. Place at the bottom of a pitcher, then pour sparkling water. Add the mint and cover. Refrigerate for at least 3 hours. Strain the liquid before serving. Add ice if desired.

20. Pomegranate Strawberry Water

This drink combines berries that are rich in antioxidant properties. It provides a sweet and fruity flavor without adding artificial sweetener.

2 cups strawberries
2 quarts (2 liter) sparkling water
½ cup pomegranate seeds

Remove the seeds from the pomegranate. Place the seeds and strawberry in a pitcher. Fill with sparkling water and ice. Refrigerate overnight. You can serve with small strawberry pieces.

21. Melon Strawberry Water

Melon and strawberries are abundant in summer, so you can get them fresh. They combine to a great metabolism booster and are very energizing.

½ watermelon
½ honeydew
2 quarts (2 liters) water
1 cup strawberries

Cut the watermelon and honeydew into small cubes. Pit the strawberries. Place in a pitcher then pour water. Chill and serve with ice if desired.

22. Hawaii Water

Pineapple has a very unique flavor that is both sweet and tangy. I got this recipe from a barkeeper on Maui, so it is a true Hawaiian water.

1 cup pineapple
½ cup coconut water
2 quarts (2 liters) spring water
½ cup lavender

Cut the pineapple into pieces. Add all ingredients in a pitcher and pour water. Place in the refrigerator for 4 hours, then serve over ice.

23. Peachy Cucumber Water

This recipe is perfect, if do not like sweet beverages. The peaches add the right amount of flavor while the cucumber makes it more refreshing.

2 peaches
1 cucumber
2 quarts (2 liters) water

Wash the fruits and slice into small pieces. Place the peaches in a pitcher, then pour the water. Add the cucumber last then cover. Refrigerate for few hours before serving. Garnish with herbs if desired.

24. Apple Mango Tropico

Tropical mango and apple makes a delicious combination. Make sure the mango is ripe to achieve the best flavor. Try to choose juicy apples as much as possible.

2 quarts (2 liters) water
1 cored apple
1 ripe mango

Rinse and core the apple and cut into cubes. Peel the mango and slightly smash it. Place in a pitcher, then pour water. Chill for 3 hours then serve with ice.

25. Blueberry Apple Water

Combining blueberries and apple tastes uniquely different from other fruit infused waters. Blueberries are rich in antioxidants, while apples are known to increase metabolism.

1 cored apple
2 cups blueberries
2 quarts (2 liters) spring water

Rinse and core the apple and chop into pieces. Slightly mash the blueberries. Place the fruits in a pitcher, then pour the water. Refrigerate for 4 hours before serving. Add ice if desired.

Section 2: Refreshing and Cooling

1. Lime Raspberry Mint Water

Raspberries taste wonderfully with lime. Mint also adds a refreshing flavor. Serve this drink with ice for a cold and sweet treat.

1 thinly sliced lime
2 cups smashed raspberries
½ cup mint
2 quarts (2 liters) filtered water

Add the berries, lime and mint in a pitcher. Pour water and place in the refrigerator for few hours. Serve with ice.

2. Cucumber Lemon Water

This is a refreshing and lemony drink that lets you cool off on a hot day. It is a great alternative to lemonade.

1 thinly sliced cucumber
2 quarts (2 liters) spring water
2 thinly sliced lemons

Add the lemon and cucumber in a pitcher and add the water. Stir then cover the pitcher. Refrigerate for 3 hours and serve cold.

3. Cranberry Orange Water

This is the perfect beverage to serve during the holidays. It has little calories and a lot of flavor.

2 quarts (2 liters) spring water
1 cup cranberries
1 thinly sliced orange
½ cup mixed herbs

Wash and drain the cranberries. Slice the orange and place it with the other ingredients in a pitcher. Pour the water and refrigerate for 3 hours. Add ice if desired.

4. Cucumber Cherry Mint

The flavor of this drink changes depending on the type of cherry you use. I recommend not using tart cherries, or the drink will lack sweetness.

2 quarts (2 liters) of spring water
1 cup pitted fresh cherries
1 thinly sliced cucumber
½ cup mint

Add the cherries, cucumber and mint in a bowl. Mash and stir, then pour the ingredients in a pitcher and add the water. Refrigerate for 3 hours and serve cold.

5. Cucumber Lavender Water

Lavender adds a light and flowery flavor to this drink.

2 quarts (2 liters) spring water
1 tsp dried or fresh lavender
1 thinly sliced cucumber

Add the lavender and cucumber in a pitcher. Pour the water and add some ice if desired. Strain first if you are using dried lavender. Serve cold.

6. Cherry Lime Water

This drink is perfect for a hot day and the gym.

2 quarts (2 liters) water
1 cup pitted fresh cherries
2 thinly sliced lime

Wash and drain the cherries. Slice the lime and place it with the pitted cherries in a pitcher. Pour water, then place in the refrigerator for 3 hours. Serve with ice if desired.

7. Kiwi Water

This kiwi water is one of my favorites, despite its simple nature.

2 quarts (2 liters) of water
4 ripe thinly sliced kiwi

Place the kiwi in a pitcher and pour the water. Refrigerate for 4 hours before serving. Garnish with kiwi chunks and ice if desired. Note: To acquire more flavor, crush the kiwi first. You can also strain the water, if you do not like to have the seeds in your drink.

8. Strawberry Cantaloupe Water

This recipe is a good substitute to fruit juice and fruit salad. Instead of the cantaloupe, you can also use any other type of melon or honeydew.

1 cup cantaloupe cubes
2 cups sliced strawberries
2 quarts (2 liters) spring water

Wash and drain the strawberries. Slice the fruits and add them to a pitcher. Pour the water and refrigerate for 3 hours. Add ice if desired

9. Pineapple Lemon Water

This drink mixes the sweetness and tangy flavor of lemon and pineapple. If you wish, you can add some honey to get a sweeter drink.

3 sliced lemons
1 cup sliced pineapple
2 quarts (2 liters) spring water
2 tbs honey (optional)

Slice the pineapple and lemon. Place in a pitcher, then add water. Add optional honey for extra sweetness. Fill with cold water and refrigerate for 3 hours. Serve with ice if desired.

10. Raspberry Lemon Water

Raspberry and lemons complement each other wonderfully to create a refreshing drink. If you wish, you can add some honey to get a sweeter drink.

2 quarts (2 liters) water
1 lemon
2 cups raspberries

Thinly slice the lemons and smash the raspberries. Place in a pitcher, pour water and refrigerate for 3 hours. Serve with ice if desired

11. Blueberry Lemon Water

Blueberry and lemon mix incredibly well together. Crush the blueberries to add more flavor.

2 quarts (2 liters) sparkling water
2 cups crushed blueberries
1 thinly sliced lemon

Place the sliced lemon and crushed blueberries in a pitcher. Pour sparkling water and add ice. Refrigerate for 3 hours before serving.

12. Mixed Berry Water

This drink incorporates 3 types of berries. It is delicious and works well on parties and other celebrations, such as New Year's Eve.

½ cup blackberries
½ cup blueberries
½ cup strawberries
2 quarts (2 liters) spring water

Slice the blueberries, strawberries and blackberries into four pieces each. Pour water into a pitcher and add the fruits. Refrigerate overnight before serving.

13. Orange Mint Water

Orange flavored water with mint content is extremely refreshing and has a natural sweetness to it.

2 quarts (2 liters) spring water
½ cup mint
1 thinly sliced orange

Thinly slice the orange and chop the mint. Combine the ingredients in a pitcher, then add the water. Set aside for 4 hours and add ice if desired.

14. Mixed Melon Water

Take advantage of the abundance of melons at the end of summer to make some mixed melon water.

1 cup honeydew pieces
1 cup cantaloupe pieces
2 quart (2 liters) spring water
1 cup watermelon pieces

Slice all of the melons and put the pieces in a pitcher. Pour water and add ice if desired. Garnish with chopped melon bits.

15. Pineapple Ginger Water

This drink is not only refreshing, it also has a sweet and spicy flavor.

1 cup pineapple pieces
2 quarts (2 liters) spring water
1 inch (2.5 cm) sliced ginger

Cut the pineapple into small pieces and thinly slice the ginger. Add the water and refrigerate for 3 hours. Serve with ice if desired.

16. Strawberry Lemon Tea

This drink combines the tanginess of lemon with the sweetness of strawberries.

2 lemons
Lemonade tea mixture
2 quarts (2 liters) spring water
10 large strawberries
Bay leaves for garnish

Boil the water and submerge the tea. Set aside for 3 minutes. Slice the strawberries and lemon and add to the pitcher. Let the mixture cool, then refrigerate for 3 hours. Add ice if desired.

17. Strawberry Mint Water

This drink has a sweet and juicy taste. The mint makes it very refreshing.

2 quarts (2 liters) spring water
2 cups strawberries
½ cup mint

Cut the strawberries into small pieces and chop the mint. Place both in a pitcher then pour the water. Refrigerate for 4 hours. Add ice before serving if desired.

18. Peach Vanilla Water

Cream and peaches tastes wonderfully together. This drink is also said to taste like dessert.

2 quarts (2 liters) spring water
1 vanilla bean
2 peaches

Wash and drain the peaches, then slice and slightly mash them. Place in the pitcher.
Slice the vanilla bean lengthwise. Scrape the seeds and add to the pitcher. Pour water on top and refrigerate for 3 hours. Add ice before serving if desired.

19. Coco Lemon Raspberry Water

Tart raspberries tend to taste less sweet, but the coconut milk makes up for it and is very healthy. Coconuts in general are among the healthiest foods in the world.

2 cups raspberries
1 lemon
½ cup coconut milk
2 quarts (2 liters) water

Thinly slice the lemons and mash the raspberries. Place the ingredients in a pitcher. Refrigerate for 3 hours. Add ice before serving if desired.

20. Ginger Orange Sprit

This sparkling water tastes a lot like orange soda and ginger juice. Experience shows that it is a great drink for people suffering from stomach pain.

2 quarts (2 liters) sparkling water
1 inch (2.5 cm) ginger
2 sliced oranges

Slice the oranges and ginger and place both in a pitcher. Add the sparkling water. Refrigerate for 4 hours before serving. Add ice if desired.

21. Cucumber Mint Water

This is a delicious and refreshing drink I often use after practicing kung fu. Apart from the mint, you can also add other herbs like rosemary and sage.

2 quarts (2 liters) spring water
1 cucumber
½ cup mint

Cut the cucumber into thin slices and chop the mint. Place all of the ingredients in a pitcher then add the water. Refrigerate for 2 hours. Add ice if desired.

22. Mango Orange Tropico

The tropical taste of mango and the citrus flavor of the orange provide a great and healthy combination. Choose a ripe mango to have a sweet flavored drink.

2 quarts (2 liters) spring water
1 sliced ripe mango
1 sliced orange

Cut the mango into small pieces and thinly slice the orange. Place the fruits in a pitcher and pour the water. Refrigerate for 4 hours. Add ice if desired.

23. Blackberry Sage Water

The blackberry in this drink provides antioxidants, while the sage causes a boost in flavor.

1 cup blackberries
½ cup sage leaves
2 quart (2 liters) spring water

Gently pit the blackberries and place in a pitcher. Pour the water, then add the sage leaves. Cover and refrigerate for 3 hours before serving. Add ice if desired.

24. Rosemary Melon Water

This combination is surprisingly delicious. The rosemary provides a subtle flavor while the watermelon makes the drink refreshing.

1 cup watermelon cubes
½ cup rosemary
2 quarts (2 liters) spring water

Remove the seeds from the watermelon, then cut into cubes. Place into a pitcher and fill with water. Add the rosemary. Refrigerate for 2 hours before serving. Strain using a wire strainer or clean mesh. Add ice if desired.

25. Strawberry Grape Water

Frozen grapes and strawberries are great to use for this recipe. It is rich in antioxidants and vitamins. The mint provides a refreshing flavor.

1 cup frozen grapes
1 cup sliced strawberries
½ cup mint
2 quarts (2 liters) spring water

Slice some of the fruits into pieces. Place in a pitcher and pour the water. Add the mint leaves, then cover. Refrigerate for 3 hours before serving. Strain using a wire strainer or clean mesh. Add ice if desired.

Section 3: Detox Drinks

1. Detox Water

Cucumbers, lemon and parsley have good detoxifying properties that can help clean the body.

1 small bunch of parsley
½ cucumber
1 quart (1 liter) spring water
½ cup frozen cranberries
1 small bunch of cilantro
1 lemon

Slice the lemon and cut the stems off the parsley and cilantro. Combine all of the ingredients in a pitcher then refrigerate. Allow it to sit overnight to intensify the flavor.

2. Gooseberry Water

This drink tastes best when it is served cold.

7 gooseberries
2 sprigs mint leaves
½ tsp lemon zest
1 tsp salt
2 quarts (2 liters) spring water
½ lemon

Remove the seeds from the gooseberry. Scoop the flesh of the fruit then add the lemon zest, water and salt. Place in a pitcher. Crush the mint leaves and add it to the lemon. Add water and refrigerate overnight. Strain the water then serve with ice if desired.

3. Cucumber Kiwi Water

This drink has a delicious fruity aftertaste and the cucumber makes it very refreshing. Try to use overripe kiwis if possible.

2 kiwis
¼ cucumber
½ lime
1 sprig of mint, diced
1 quart (1 liter) spring water

Slice the cucumber into thin slices and dice the mint. Combine the ingredients in a pitcher, then add water. Place in the refrigerator overnight. Serve with ice if desired.

4. Cucumber Melon Water

Cucumber and melon provide a summery taste. The honeydew also adds a good amount of natural sweetness.

1 cucumber
¼ cantaloupe
½ honeydew
2 quarts (2 liters) spring water

Wash and drain the fruits. Cut the cucumber into thin slices. Chop the honeydew and cantaloupe into large cubes. Place in a pitcher then pour water. Refrigerate for 3 hours. You can garnish with melon bits and add ice if desired.

5. Strawberry Kiwi Classic

Strawberry and kiwi is a classic combination for fruit infused water. Kiwi contains Vitamin A and Vitamin E, which can help to clean your colon and improve your overall wellbeing.

2 kiwis
2 strawberries
1 quart (1 liter) spring water

Dice the ingredients and place in a pitcher. Add water then refrigerate for 4 hours. Strain the water before serving. Add ice if desired.

6. Minty Melon Water

This watermelon mint water is considered as one of the easiest and best detox drinks available. Watermelon contains citrulline which improves liver function by removing ammonia and repairing damage cells.

3 mint leaves
½ cup cubed watermelon
1 quart (1 liter) spring water

Cut the watermelon into cubes and place all ingredients in a pitcher. Add the water, then refrigerate overnight. Strain the water before serving. Add ice if desired.

7. Cleansing Lemon Ginger Water

Ginger has anti-oxidant properties and can aid in your digestion. Lemon, on the other hand, helps to neutralize the free radicals in your body.

1 lemon
½ cup mint leaves
½ cucumber
¼ ginger root
1 quart (1 liter) spring water

Wash and drain the ingredients. Cut the cucumber into thin slices and grate the ginger into small pieces. Place in a pitcher, then add water. Refrigerate before serving. You can keep refilling the pitcher with water several times before you need to replace the ingredients.

8. Coco Berry Water

Berries tend to taste better when served in sparkling water. Raspberries contain phytochemicals that have anti-cancer and anti-ageing agents. Coconut is one of the healthiest foods in the world and has hundreds of benefits.

½ cup blackberries
½ cup raspberries
½ cup coconut milk
1 quart (1 liter) sparkling water

Wash the berries and set aside. Pour water into a pitcher. Cut some of the berries but leave most of them whole. Add to the water. Set aside for few hours before serving. Add is if desired.

9. Pomegranate Lemon Pineapple Water

Pomegranate is a great fruit for detox therapy. It has potent anti-cancer elements and can also reduce the risk of heart ailments and stroke.

1 cup chopped pineapple
1 pint (½ liter) spring water
1 inch (2.5 cm) ginger
½ cup pomegranate
½ lemon

Wash and drain the fruits. Cut into thin and small pieces. Mix all of the ingredients in a pitcher, then refrigerate for 3 hours. Serve with ice if desired.

10. Mango Pineapple Tropico

This tropical mango recipe has a sweet taste and is among my favorites after working out.

1 cup frozen mango
1 cup pineapple
1 quart (1 liter) spring water

Wash and drain the fruits. Cut the mangos into chunks. Pour the water in a pitcher and add the fruits. Refrigerate for 5 hours before serving. You can also include small bits of mango into your drink and add ice if you desire.

11. Hydrating Fruit Mix

Hydrating fruits like cucumbers are perfect for detoxification, since it can help flush toxins out of the body. As an additional bonus, it also serves as a very refreshing drink on a hot day.

3 organic cucumbers, sliced
2 apples
Mint to taste
½ cup organic strawberries
2 quarts (2 liters) spring water

Wash and drain the fruits. Cut the cucumbers into thin slices. Cut the apples into quarter pieces. Place the ingredients in a pitcher, then pour the water. Place in the refrigerator for 3 hours before serving. You can garnish with fresh strawberries. Add ice if desired.

12. Green Citrus Water

The main idea of drinking detox water is to feel cleansed and rejuvenated. You can add a small amount of honey for flavor, but do not go overboard or it will overpower the citrus flavor. As an alternative, you can use coconut milk instead.

1 grapefruit
½ banana
½ tbs honey (optional)
1 orange
2 quarts (2 liters) of spring water

Slice the banana into thin slices. Smash the grapefruit and orange. Place all of the ingredients in a pitcher. Refrigerate for 3 hours before serving. Add ice if desired.

13. Red and Green Water

This recipe has great detoxifying properties that can remove free radicals while providing the body with essential nutrients.

1 cup pomegranate
1 cup frozen cranberries
1 pitted pear
6 mint leaves
1 inch (2.5 cm) ginger
4 kale leaves
2 quarts (2 liters) spring water

Wash and drain the ingredients. Slice fruits and ginger into slices. Place all ingredients in a pitcher, then pour water. Refrigerate for 4 hours before serving. Add ice if desired.

14. Grapefruit Sunrise

This is a great detox water after drinking alcohol on festivities. It has a sweet and tangy taste.

½ avocado
1 cup fresh grapefruit
¾ cup banana
½ cup orange
1 cup strawberries
1 quart (1 liter) spring water

Cut the grapefruit into small pieces. Slice the strawberries and banana. Place the fruits in a pitcher, then pour the water. Refrigerate for 3 hours. Serve with garnish and add ice if desired.

15 Detox Blueberry Water

This detoxifying water is perfect for flushing out your system and acquiring necessary nutrients. You can also add coconut milk into this recipe.

½ cup frozen blueberries
1 banana
¼ cup cranberry
½ coconut milk (optional)
1 quart (1 liter) sparkling water

Wash and drain the fruits. Slice the bananas thinly and smash the cranberries slightly. Place the fruits at the bottom of a pitcher, then pour sparkling water. Refrigerate overnight and serve with ice if desired.

16. Orange Vegetable Water

The apples used in this drink provide a sweet base. The carrots add a vibrant color, while the celery and lime add a salty taste.

2 apples
1 celery stalk
2 medium carrots
4 lime
1 quart (1 liter) spring water

Wash and drain the ingredients. Slice the apples into four pieces each. Remove the top of the carrots. Cut the carrots and celery into pieces.
Place the apples, carrots and celery in a pitcher and pour water. Cut the limes then add to the pitcher. Refrigerate for 4 hours before serving. Add ice if desired.

17. Liver Detox Water

This detox drink promotes the flow of fat and bile in your body. Cleaning the liver is an important step in increasing metabolism and detoxification in the body. Caring for your liver is especially important if you drink alcohol.

2 medium beets
1 lemon
1 red apple
1 inch (2.5 cm) ginger
2 quarts (2 liters) spring water

Slice the lemon thinly. Chop the red apple into chunks, then grate the ginger. Place the ingredients in a pitcher and water. Refrigerate for 3 hours. Strain the water before serving. Add ice if desired.

18. Beet Water

This drink is a good replacement for sugary juices. Beets are naturally sweet and rich in nutrients.

2 raw beets
1 banana
½ cup strawberries
1 lime
½ cup pineapple
3 quarts (3 liters) spring water

Wash the beets and peel. Remove the leaves and stem. Chop the pineapple, banana and strawberries. Cut the lime into wedges. Place the fruits in a pitcher. Pour water. Refrigerate for at least 3 hours before serving. Add ice if desired.

19. Citrus Banana Water

This is one of the most popular fruit infused water recipes I know. It has a cool and refreshing taste that is perfect on hot days. The lime, lemons and tangerines add the right amount of sweetness and tanginess.

2 oranges
4 bananas
1 lime
2 tangerines
1 lemon
2 quarts (2 liters) spring water

Rinse and peel the fruits. Slice the citrus fruits thinly. Chop the bananas. Place the fruits in a pitcher. Pour water. Place in the refrigerator overnight to infuse the flavors properly. You can garnish your drink with lemon or lime wedges and add ice if desired.

20. Green Lemon Water

The flavor of this drink can be intense, so feel free to reduce some of the ingredients and gradually add them later on.

1 apple
½ lemon
½ inch (1.25 cm) ginger
2 quarts (2 liters) spring water

Wash and drain the fruits. Chop the apples into chunks. Grate the ginger and slice the lemon into wedges. Place in a pitcher, then add water. Set aside for 3 hours before serving. Add ice if desired.

21. Cranberry Detox Water

Cranberries can help reduce bloating. This drink is beneficial after festivities. It contains anti-inflammatory properties and antiseptic agents that can serve as a natural detoxifier.

2 apples
1 lemon
2 pears
1 cup fresh cranberries
2 quarts (2 liters) spring water

Wash the apple and pears then chop into large chunks. Peel the lemon and cut into quarters. Remember to remove the seeds. Place the fruits in a pitcher. Pour water. Refrigerate for 4 hours. Add ice if desired.

22. Vinegar Detox Water

Apple cider vinegar can help eliminate toxins effectively. It also breaks the mucus in the body and aids digestion. Lemon stimulates gastric juice and also helps break down fat correctly. You can drink this water every morning.

1/2 cup apple cider vinegar
2 apples
1 lemon
1 cinnamon stick (optional)
2 quart (2 liter) sparkling water

Wash and drain the apples. Cut the apples and slice the lemon into thin wedges. Place into a pitcher and pour water. Add a cinnamon stick if desired. Refrigerate for 4 hours before serving. Add ice if desired.

23. Ginger Detox Water

Ginger is a powerful detoxifier that can help increase your metabolism. Lemons are also considered to be a detoxifier, since they have a natural diuretic effect that helps to remove toxins from your body.

2 lemon
2 inch (5 cm) ginger root
1 quart (1 liter) spring water

Grate the ginger and cut the lemon into wedges, then add them to a pitcher. Refrigerate for 3 hours before serving. Add ice if desired.

24. Cucumber Citrus Water

Citrus and cucumber blend wonderfully. You can serve this drink on parties as a replacement to sugar filled juice.

1 lemon
1 orange
1 lime
1 cucumber
2 quarts (2 liters) spring water

Wash and drain the fruits. Cut into thin slices. Place the fruits in a pitcher, then add half gallon of water. Refrigerate for 3 hours before serving. Add ice if desired.

25. Orange Coco water

Orange is rich in vitamin C, which can increase immunity against free radicals. Mint provides a wonderful and refreshing flavor and coconuts are among the healthiest foods in the world.

10 mint leaves
1 sliced orange
1 cup of coconut milk
2 quart (2 liter) spring water

Place the mint and orange slices in a pitcher. Pour the water and coconut milk. Refrigerate for 3 hours before serving. Garnish with orange slice and add ice if desired.

26. Basil Melon Water

This is a great detox recipe for the end of summer, not only for the refreshing nature of watermelons, but since you can get them fresh in that time of the year.

2 cups watermelon
10 basil leaves
2 quarts (2 liters) spring water

Remove the seeds from the watermelon, then cut it into cubes. Place the ingredients in a pitcher. Refrigerate for 3 hours. You can garnish with basil sprigs and add ice if desired.

27. Cilantro Citrus Water

This recipe is rich in citrus fruits and thus vitamin C. The coriander adds a taste of sweetness to this drink, while the citrus adds tanginess.

1 lemon
1 orange
1 lime
¼ cup cilantro
2 quarts (2 liters) spring water

Prepare the fruits by slicing them. Place all ingredients in a pitcher and pour water. Refrigerate for 3 hours, then serve with ice if desired. Garnish with orange slices and herbs.

28. Lavender Lemon Water

Lavender has a soothing effect. The lemon add a citrus flavor and vitamin C.

3 lemons
¼ cup fresh lavender
2 quarts (2 liters) spring water

Slice the lemons, then cut the lavender. Place all ingredients in a pitcher and pour water. Refrigerate for at least 3 hours to allow the flavors to infuse. Garnish with lavender and add ice if desired.

29. Pineapple Chipotle Tea

Pineapple has a very strong flavor, while mint adds a refreshing touch to the drink. This is a good replacement to alcoholic beach drinks.

¼ cup water
10 mint leaves
2 cups cubed pineapple
2 quarts (2 liters) spring water
¼ tsp dried chipotle
2 tsp honey (optional)

Mix the optional honey and water in a pot. Bring the water into a boil. Reduce to a simmer for 3 minutes or until the water thickens. Remove from heat, then set aside.
Pour the mix into a glass with the mint and chipotle leaves. Add the pineapple and stir to combine. Refrigerate the mixture for 5 hours. Garnish with sliced pineapple and mint. Add ice if desired.

30. Cherry Banana Water (Kiba)

I learned this recipe in Germany, where they call it "Kiba". It is a general name used for a mixture of cherry juice and banana nectar, which I highly recommend, by the way.

2 bananas
2 cups cherries
2 quarts (2 liters) spring water

Slice the bananas and mash them a bit. Pit the cherries. Place both ingredients in a pitcher, then pour water. Refrigerate the mixture for 5 hours. Add ice if desired.

Made in the USA
Middletown, DE
13 April 2016